EXPLOSION OF LIFE

By the same author:

Evangelism by Fire
Mighty Manifestations
The Assurance of Salvation
The Secret of the Blood of Jesus
How to Receive a Miracle from God
The Baptism in the Holy Spirit
Now that You are Saved
From Minus to Plus
The Ultimate Plus

EXPLOSION OF LIFE

The World Drama of Resurrection

REINHARD BONNKE

Hodder & Stoughton
LONDON SYDNEY AUCKLAND

Copyright © 1994 by Reinhard Bonnke

The right of Reinhard Bonnke to be identified as the Author of the Work has been asserted by him in accordance with the Copyright, Designs and Patents Act 1988.

Edited by Simon Jenkins

10 9 8 7 6 5 4 3 2 1

All rights reserved. No part of this publication may be reproduced, stored in a retrieval system, or transmitted, in any form or by any means without the prior written permission of the publisher, nor be otherwise circulated in any form of binding or cover other than that in which it is published and without a similar condition being imposed on the subsequent purchaser.

British Library Cataloguing in Publication Data

A catalogue record for this book is available from the British Library

Typeset by Hewer Text Composition Services, Edinburgh
Printed and bound in Great Britain by
Cox & Wyman Ltd, Reading, Berks

Hodder and Stoughton Ltd
A Division of Hodder Headline PLC
338 Euston Road
London NW1 3BH

Contents

The Message of Resurrection	9
The Resurrection Now	17
An Excursion through the Bible	23
A Death that Really Happened	29
'I am the resurrection'	41
Explosion of Life	51

The Message of Resurrection

Joseph had never been to Jerusalem before. He had travelled by ship, and then on foot, from his home in Cyprus to join thousands of other pilgrims at one of the most popular Jewish feasts – the joyful feast of Pentecost.

The streets were packed with pilgrims. The bazaar was doing a roaring trade. The whole city was full of the cries of streetsellers, the tramp of feet and the buzz of the crowds. But that morning, Joseph ignored it all. Instead, he headed straight for the heart of the city and gazed upon the fabled splendours of King Herod's great temple for the first time.

That year, AD 30, Joseph had become a 'God-fearer' – a converted Jew. As he stood in the early morning sunlight and watched the temple's ornate ritual, with its colourful Hebrew music and the odours of incense and sacrifice, he hoped to be blessed by God and find spiritual satisfaction.

Explosion of Life

As he left the temple, he noticed crowds of people running. At first he hesitated, but then his curiosity got the better of him and he followed them. A minute later, he was at the back of a large crowd standing in an open space. Facing them on the flat rooftop of a grand house was a large group of people, men and women. A big figure with a strong northern accent – he was obviously from Galilee – and a resonant voice was speaking with passion and eloquence. Joseph pushed his way to the front. He had missed the beginning, but whatever the speaker was saying, it had electrified the crowd.

What he heard next were the most astonishing words in all his life. Not only was he startled, but a visible and audible ripple of almost shocked wonder or perhaps fear disturbed the crowd.

Listen to these words, fellow Israelites! Jesus of Nazareth was a man whose divine authority was clearly proven to you by all the miracles and wonders which God performed through him. You yourselves know this, for it happened here among you. In accordance with his own plan God had already decided that Jesus would be handed over to you; and you killed him by letting sinful men crucify him. But God raised him from death, setting him free from its power, because it was impossible that death should hold him prisoner. (Acts 2:22–24)

Resurrection! Joseph had heard the first public declaration that Jesus Christ had been raised from the dead. He was present at the very beginning of the Christian faith. That day he became a 'follower of the Way' himself, along with some three thousand others in the crowd.

The doors of history were beginning to move. The world was about to change.

BEGINNING WITH MARY

Joseph later heard story after story about what had happened on the morning of the resurrection. He learned that the first to know of this tremendous event was a follower of Jesus named Mary, from the lakeside town of Magdala.

Mary Magdalene had become one of Jesus' most devoted followers. Until she met him, Mary's life had been something of a war zone – she was possessed by seven fractious devils which drove her in seven different directions. Jesus had cast them all out of her. She was there at the cross when Jesus died, and she was the first at the tomb on Easter morning.

After Jesus had been pronounced dead, his body had been wrapped in linen and placed in a rock cavity cut in the face of the cliff. The Romans who had crucified Jesus set a guard on the tomb to keep away troublemakers. Since that time, Mary had returned constantly to the tomb, and had scarcely slept.

After her second night of grief, she left her house again, heading for the tomb in the hour before dawn. True, only a certain kind of woman would be in the streets when it was dark, but with her past she had no reputation to worry about.

'WOMAN, WHY ARE YOU CRYING?'

When she arrived in the garden, Mary was shocked. The soldiers were nowhere to be seen. The stone was rolled back. The entrance to the tomb was open. Had the grave been violated? Had even his body gone? Numbed, she stood there trembling, until somebody came up behind her.

'Woman, why are you crying?' a man's voice asked her.

Turning, Mary saw a figure standing in the half-light. It must be the gardener, she thought. So she said to him: 'If you took him away, sir, tell me where you have put him, and I will go and get him.'

He did not reply, and so she turned back to face the tomb.

Then again the voice spoke. Just one word: 'Mary!' It was the perfect imitation of the voice of Jesus – but it could not be him, she was sure. He was dead. Yet nobody else ever had a voice like that. Confused and frightened, she slowly turned round again and a streak of light broke through the trees and showed her who it was. Her heart almost convulsed with the greatest joy any human being had ever experienced. It *was* him.

She fell before him with a cry of 'Teacher!' He told her, 'Don't hold on to me – I am not leaving you yet!' And then he told her to tell the good news to his disciples.

She ran to tell Peter and the rest. At first they did not believe her. Her story was too incredible – and too good – to be true (see John 20:11–18). But that evening, Jesus himself appeared to them too. And over the next six weeks he was seen by hundreds of people – leaving no possible doubt. Jesus had certainly died, but he was now most certainly alive.

THE RESURRECTION THEN

About the year AD 55, a man boarded a ship in one of the major ports of the Roman world – the city of Ephesus. In a leather bag over his shoulder he carried a letter that was to become world-famous.

This unknown messenger was heading for the city of Corinth, a seaport of proverbial immorality, and the centre for the worship of Aphrodite, the goddess of love. A few years earlier, a Christian church had been planted in this unlikely spot, and it was to these

Explosion of Life

Christians that the letter carried by the messenger was addressed. It carried the signature of Paul, the apostle to both Jews and ethnic peoples in Asia Minor and Europe. Paul's letter was hard-hitting. It was written to correct some major problems among the Christians in Corinth. But it also included a great statement of what the Christian faith truly is.

And now I want to remind you, my brothers, of the good news which I preached to you, which you received, and on which your faith stands firm. You are saved by the gospel if you hold firmly to it.

I passed on to you what I received, which is of the greatest importance: that Christ died for our sins, as written in the Scriptures; that he was buried and that he was raised to life on the third day, as written in the Scriptures.

This is what we all preach, and this is what you believe. (1 Cor 15:1–4; 11)

Three hundred years after Paul's letter had been delivered in Corinth, the Roman empire had officially accepted these beliefs. Many thousands of people had realised that events of global significance had taken place in the life of Jesus. Christ had come, he had been crucified and had been raised from the dead. *His coming distinguished this planet.* Nothing could ever be the same again. His own followers were so affected by it that they became like *human pieces of evidence*. Evidence that can still point us to the reality and power of Jesus himself.

The Resurrection Now

In the year 1992, in a northern English city, a newspaper journalist asked a group of twenty young people what Easter meant to them. One connected it with Jesus Christ, and another, a Roman Catholic, knew it was when Christ died and rose from the dead. The rest had no idea what Easter meant – except that it was a holiday. Their lives were a spiritual vacuum. Easter had become only 'a chance for a rave'.

Going by this straw poll, ninety per cent of young people are ignorant of the world's greatest event! What hope is there for the future of our society? Add to it the millions who say 'I'm not the religious type' – as if this was a virtue – and where does all this land us?

Religious indifference has a saw edge – it is cutting off the branch on which our culture is sitting.

Explosion of Life

WHAT COULDN'T HAPPEN, DID HAPPEN

Paul the apostle posed a question which to this day nobody has succeeded in answering: 'Why should any of you consider it incredible that God raises the dead?' (Acts 26:8).

The resurrection of Christ has always been controversial. Paul said that by the death and resurrection of Christ, 'God has shown that this world's wisdom is foolishness!' (1 Cor 1:20). He knew what he was talking about. Paul was familiar with the philosophers of Greece. He had argued with them when he arrived in Athens and had made his way to the city's debating ground.

After 600 years of Greek thought and religion, Paul looked around and found an altar to 'the unknown god'. Six centuries of genius and God still unknown! The all-important knowledge had eluded them.

Paul said, 'That which you worship, even though you do not know it, is what I now proclaim to you' (Acts 17:23). Paul's accusation, that his learned listeners 'did not know' God, must have stung. But it was true. Some equated God with happiness, *'the good'*, or even the state. To one Greek thinker, God was a triangle, and his chief rule was not to eat beans!

Intellect has proved the wrong instrument with which to contact God. Today, 2,000 years later, thinkers are certain of nothing – except that nothing is certain. Many of them have doubted their own existence. What does that do for us?

DISCARD THE RESURRECTION?

The New Testament exists to proclaim the resurrection of Christ. We either acknowledge that Christ is risen, and that he is the living Christ, or else we have to scrap the New Testament. But where will we find some other dynamic for our culture?

Suppose the resurrection didn't happen and we drop the Bible into the wastepaper basket – what then? Every church on earth would be closed. All praying would have to stop, and no hymn, no psalm, no oratorio, would ever be sung again. Who would sanction the great Christian principles, maxims and moral code? They would carry no authority.

On top of all that, the love, service, sacrifice and dedication of untold hundreds of millions would have to be seen as a vast and futile mistake. The conversion of multitudes, miracle-healings, wonderful answers to prayer, and every witness to encountering God – all of them would have to be written off as an illusion. The saints and martyrs tortured to death would have been deceived. The great religious pioneers, from Athanasius to Livingstone, from Luther to Billy Graham, would have wasted their lives.

Explosion of Life

The brilliant Christian thinkers, from Augustine to Pascal and Newton, together with the army of Christian scholars, teachers, preachers and students – all would have been fooled. Is that possible?

The apostle Paul put it bluntly. He said that if Christ is not risen then 'we are of all men most miserable'. He suffered more for witnessing to the resurrection of Christ than almost anyone, and he knew if Christ was still dead, it would all have been pain in vain. This is what he says:

If Christ has not been raised, our preaching is useless and so is your faith. More than that, we are then found to be false witnesses about God, for we have testified about God that he raised Christ from the dead. If Christ has not been raised, your faith is futile, you are still in your sins. Then those who have fallen asleep in Christ are lost. If only for this life we have hope in Christ, we are to be pitied more than all men. (1 Cor 15:14–15; 17–19)

The terrifying disillusionment which Paul describes is too great a nightmare to ponder. The dedication and love of almost a hundred generations of men and women could never be inspired by a baseless myth that had no foundation in reality. Through the centuries, people have truly known the ever-present

Christ, or else the heavens and earth are composed of a lie. As Paul went on to say: 'But the truth is that Christ has been raised from death' (1 Cor 15:20).

An Excursion through the Bible

Christianity does not rest on debate. Reason can take us some of the way towards the truth, but in the end, only faith and the power of God can bring us into the light. This means that it is not only important to think through our faith, but also to seek God's help for what we cannot fully understand.

The apostle Paul said, 'My message and my preaching were not with wise and persuasive words, but with a demonstration of the Spirit's power, so that your faith might not rest on man's wisdom, but on God's power' (1 Cor 2:4–5).

The resurrection of Christ is the Christian faith. It is the substance of the whole New Testament. We can see this by going on a short excursion through its pages.

Explosion of Life

In the four Gospels – *Matthew, Mark, Luke* and *John* – the resurrection is mentioned long before it even happened. Before he was arrested and crucified, Jesus told his disciples that he would suffer, be put to death and rise again. For instance, he compared himself to the Old Testament prophet Jonah: 'For as Jonah was three days and three nights in the belly of a huge fish, so the Son of Man will be three days and three nights in the heart of the earth' (Matt 12:40). That is where Jesus was, from sunset on the 15th of the Jewish month Nisan, to daybreak on the 17th.

The Gospel of *John* is full of resurrection truths. It peaks at great statements like 'I am the resurrection and the life' (John 11:25). It gives many examples of his appearances after his resurrection – all of them with the ring of truth, carrying the hallmarks of eye-witness experience.

The book of *Acts* starts with the resurrection. In an almost matter-of-fact way it states that Jesus appeared to his followers over a period of forty days and spoke to them about the kingdom of God. The entire twenty-eight chapters of Acts paint a vivid picture of thirty years of Christ's activity after the resurrection.

The book of *Romans*, the greatest theological work of all time, would simply fall apart without the resurrection. In it Paul says, 'I am not ashamed of the gospel [the good news of the resurrection], because it is the power of God for the salvation of everyone who believes' (Rom. 1:16).

In *1 Corinthians,* Paul gives instructions about the Eucharist or 'the Lord's supper'. Paul says that we eat this meal not in memory of a dead hero, but of a living Lord. By eating the bread and drinking the wine, Paul says, 'you proclaim the Lord's death until he comes' (1 Cor 11:26). Dead men don't come back!

Even in the most ordinary phrases, Jesus is taken to be alive. Paul mentions this almost in passing in his words of blessing to his Christian readers. For example in *Galatians*: 'The grace of our Lord Jesus Christ be with your spirit, brothers. Amen' (Gal 6:18). A dead man's grace is worth nothing!

In his letter to the *Ephesians*, Paul sees the resurrection as far more than a mere event in the past. His thought expands so that the resurrection is seen as an almighty explosion of God's power, which sets us free:

That power is like the working of his mighty strength, which he exerted in Christ when he raised him from the dead and seated him at his right hand in the heavenly realms, far above all rule and authority, power and dominion, and every title that can be given. And God placed all things under his feet and appointed him to be head over everything for the church, which is his body, the fullness of him who fills everything in every way. (Eph 1:19–23)

Explosion of Life

No one could pen such words about something that never happened. A bit of magic inspires no such lofty thoughts.

Paul sent several short letters to churches in Asia Minor (modern-day Turkey) and Greece. In them he says that Christ was not merely raised from the dead, but was raised to the highest place in heaven and earth, to God's right hand, at the centre of all existence (see Phil 2:5–11). This is not merely an inspiring vision of where Christ is now. The point of it is that God has exalted Christ so that everyone who has ever existed will ultimately acknowledge Jesus as Lord of the universe. No greater vision of hope has ever been given to us.

The book of *James* was written by the half-brother of Jesus. He was a down-to-earth type. When Jesus began his ministry, James and the rest of Jesus' family in Nazareth thought that Jesus was going mad. They even tracked him down to try to bring him back home. But after the resurrection, even James was brought to the feet of Christ. Paul tells us that when Jesus rose from the dead, he appeared to James (1 Cor 15:7). James is proud to call himself 'a servant of God and of the Lord Jesus Christ' (Jas 1:1).

Reinhard Bonnke

THE WITNESS OF ST JOHN

The apostle John, the disciple who was closest to Jesus, wrote a Gospel, three letters, and also the book of Revelation. John's letters powerfully trumpet the resurrection note. And the book of Revelation is a total endorsement of the truth that Christ lives in supreme glory and power. In this final book of the Bible, John, exiled for his faith on the Greek island of Patmos, has a series of awesome revelations. He sees Christ on the throne of the universe. Multitudes surround it, singing 'Worthy is the Lamb, who was slain, to receive power and wealth and wisdom and strength and honour and glory and praise!' (Rev. 5:12).

Christ is the fact behind all facts. It brought John not merely to his knees but to fall on his face in wonder. Writing some thirty or forty years after the crucifixion, John describes how he saw Jesus:

His head and hair were white like wool, as white as snow, and his eyes were like blazing fire. His feet were like bronze glowing in a furnace, and his voice was like the sound of rushing waters. His face was like the sun shining in all its brilliance.

When I saw him, I fell at his feet as though dead. Then he placed his right hand on me and said: 'Do not be afraid. I am the First and the Last. I am the Living One; I was dead, and behold

Explosion of Life

I am alive for ever and ever! And I hold the keys of death and Hades.' (Rev 1:14–18)

In this remarkable book, God is called 'He who was, and is, and is to come' (Rev 4:8). We might have expected it to say 'He who was, and is, and who will be' – but God is not a 'will be' God! He is not the great 'I will be', but the great 'I am'. Not a phantom figure of the indefinite future, 'beyond the bright blue sky', but the God who deals with us all our lives.

As another part of the New Testament puts it: 'Jesus Christ is the same yesterday and today and for ever' (Heb 13:8). The words of Revelation are in the present and continuous tense, like a river that flows on for ever. A river of grace, salvation and life.

It is the resurrection which leads us to this wonderful vision of God. The resurrection is not just a one-off happening. It is not Christ alive for forty days – and then vanishing. Instead, it means that Jesus is ever-present with us, bringing all that God longs to pour out on us – freedom from sin, healing, forgiveness, and life in all its fullness.

A Death that Really Happened

Alongside the resurrection, the death of Christ is the foundation of the New Testament. The two events go together in showing us what Jesus came to do. Paul's summary of the good news of Jesus was that 'Christ died for our sins, as written in the Scriptures; that he was buried and that he was raised to life three days later, as written in the Scriptures' (1 Cor 15:3–4). Paul's strong emphasis on the fact that Jesus was dead and buried – it is almost as if he is underlining the words in his letter – is very important, as we will see in a moment.

The resurrection has had many critics, and some of them have suggested that Jesus never rose from the dead because he never died. This accusation has been around for a long time. Modern critics have said that Jesus was crucified, but that he fainted on the cross and was taken down before he was dead. According to one theory, Jesus revived in the coolness of the tomb

Explosion of Life

and let himself out. Another theory has it that the disciples snatched him from the tomb and nursed him back to health.

There is not a scrap of evidence for these desperate theories. They raise more questions than they answer. For example:

How did the Roman soldiers – experienced and efficient executioners – mistake Jesus for dead?

How did Jesus survive the shock and exposure of the crucifixion, followed by some thirty-six hours in a cold tomb, without any medical attention?

How could a man in that condition shift a stone weighing a quarter of a ton from the door to get out?

How could this limping, wounded Jesus pass himself off to the disciples as the glorious risen Lord?

Or if the disciples rescued Jesus to pretend that he had risen from the dead, why did they never produce him publicly to prove it?

If the resurrection was some kind of con trick on the general public, it is very hard to see why the disciples did it. They never gained a penny by it – instead, it cost them life-long persecution and, for most of them, martyrdom. Simon Peter, Andrew, James, Paul – they were all put to death proclaiming the truth of the resurrection, and neither threats, imprisonment nor torture could change their story. They knew it was true and that it would change the world – which it did.

THE EVENTS OF JESUS' DEATH

It is worth taking some time to think about the death of Jesus. It is important to understand how it happened and what it means.

Jesus' enemies wanted his death – and they worked hard to engineer it. These religious leaders hated Jesus because he challenged their hypocrisy and corruption and threatened their privileged position. In the end, they only got what they wanted by blackmailing Pontius Pilate, the Roman procurator, into signing Jesus' death warrant.

Once Jesus had been crucified, a wealthy and influential man called Joseph, from the town of Arimathea, asked Pilate if he could give the body of Jesus a proper burial. Joseph, however, was a known Jesus sympathiser. He was the last person to be trusted with the body if there was the slightest chance that it might not stay put in the grave. Pilate wanted Jesus' death certified first. The centurion leading the execution

Explosion of Life

squad guaranteed that Jesus was dead, and he gave proof of it. It happened like this.

The crucifixion took place on the day before the Passover, the most sacred feast of the whole Jewish year. The holy day began at sunset on the day Jesus was crucified. No executed man was allowed to stay hanging after sunset, especially in the holy city of Jerusalem, so to hasten their end the soldiers broke the legs of the criminals who were crucified with Jesus. This cramped their breathing and quickly brought their agonies to an end through asphyxiation.

However, to their surprise, they found that Jesus was already dead. They couldn't quite believe this, so they made absolutely sure. A soldier stabbed a spear deep into Jesus' heart through his rib cage. The bystanders saw a gush of blood and water flow from his body.

John's Gospel records all this in detail (in John 19:31–37). And John, who was present at the crucifixion, adds these words to his description of the event: 'The one who saw this happen has spoken of it, so that you also may believe' (John 19:35). Jesus was truly dead. This is vitally important, because it is his death which brings us new life and which defeats the power of death itself.

Joseph, together with his friend Nicodemus, received the body of Jesus and prepared it for burial with embalming spices and linen winding cloths. Then they carried him down to the little tomb, which was in the same spur of rock which formed the execution ground.

At the request of the priests, Pilate ordered that soldiers should be put on guard duty to prevent the grave being robbed by the devoted followers of Christ. The tomb was sealed, possibly with a rope across the heavy stone which blocked the mouth of the tomb.

Two women, Mary the mother of Jesus, and Mary Magdalene, watched while the body was put there. On the preparation day before the Sabbath they also brought spices for his body.

BOASTING IN THE CROSS

The disciples knew that Jesus was dead. They were shattered by these terrifying events. But after his resurrection, they came to see what it all meant. And they insisted, more than ever, that Jesus had truly died, and that he was truly raised from death. They preached his death, together with the resurrection, as the heart of the Christian good news. The cross, a symbol of shame, terror and suffering, became their glory and the focus of their preaching. We can see this all through the New Testament:

May I never boast except in the cross of our Lord Jesus Christ, through which the world has been crucified to me, and I to the world. (Gal 6:14)

Explosion of Life

Christ became a man and appeared in human likeness. He was humble and walked the path of obedience all the way to death – his death on the cross. (Phil 2:7–8)

Let us fix our eyes on Jesus, the author and perfecter of our faith, who for the joy set before him endured the cross, scorning its shame, and sat down at the right hand of the throne of God. (Heb 12:2)

The great symbol of the Christian faith is the cross. It could also be symbolized by an empty tomb, although that is not so easily pictured. The disciples preached the good news that Jesus had risen, but they also saw his death as good news – declaring that Jesus laid down his life to save the world. This must have been a difficult message to preach. Following a crucified leader was not much to be proud of. Crucifixion was so shameful and obscene that people considered it indecent even to talk about it.

In the Roman town of Pompeii, a piece of graffiti sketched on a wall and preserved from the first century shows a crucified man with the head of a donkey. A figure is praying in front of it. A Latin sentence scrawled underneath mocks this member of the household staff as 'praying to his god'.

But the disciples of Jesus were not ashamed of his death. Instead, the death of Christ became with the resurrection the central truth which they proclaimed. This is how it must always be. It is the hallmark of a real Saviour. He died for our sins in the strange blackness of that terrible afternoon long ago. If he only fainted and did not die then he did not bear our sins. But he did die, and he lives to save us. That Friday will always be known as Good Friday.

HOW JESUS SAW HIS DEATH

Jesus himself always knew he must suffer a violent death. He saw it not as an accident, or a terrible twist of fate, but as the whole point of what he had come to do. This is what he said about his death:

The Son of Man did not come to be served, but to serve, and to give his life as a ransom for many. (Mark 10:45)

I am the good shepherd. The good shepherd lays down his life for the sheep. The reason my Father loves me is that I lay down my life – only to take it up again. (John 10:11, 17)

I am the living bread that came down from heaven. If anyone eats of this bread he will live for ever. This bread is my flesh, which I will give for the life of the world. (John 6:51)

At one stage, Jesus spelt out to the disciples exactly what was going to happen. He told them: 'I must go to Jerusalem and suffer much from the elders, the chief priests, and the teachers of the Law. I will be put to death, but on the third day I will be raised to life' (Matt 16:21). This devastated the disciples. Peter confronted Jesus. 'Never, Lord!' he said. 'This shall not happen to you.' Jesus' response to Peter shows how he saw his coming death. He immediately recognised Peter's words as a temptation inspired by Satan to avoid the way of the cross. 'Get away from me, Satan!' Jesus said. 'You are an obstacle in my way, because these thoughts of yours don't come from God, but from man' (Matt 16:23). Anything that stopped Jesus from going to the cross was Satanic. There was simply no other way for Jesus to complete the work God had given him to do. There was no other way to rescue us from our sin.

In John's Gospel, Jesus says: 'But I, when I am lifted up from the earth, will draw all men to myself.' And John adds these words: 'He said this is to show the kind of death he was going to die' (John 12:32–3).

The preaching of Christ lifted up to die, and raised up by God, lifts men and women like no other force on earth. It lifts people's hearts; lifts up their heads. It lifts the sombre veil of oppression that shrouds men and women. It sets people free.

DEAD OR ALIVE?

Jesus certainly died for our sins, but a forever dead Christ would be no use. That is what his enemies wanted – a silenced, useless Jesus. If he was dead his voice would never speak against them. His hands with nails through them would heal no sick people. His feet would not take him anywhere once they were fastened down with iron spikes. A dead Jesus is a Jesus who never saves, never heals, never casts out demons. It is a dead religion. I have been in churches where I almost looked around expecting to see a coffin with a dead Jesus in it. It seemed as if the people were mourning the dead. In those churches they had a useless Jesus, who never did anything, just as if he was in a tomb – in the night 'when no man can work', as he once described it.

Some preach a Jesus who is almost unrecognisable. He never does anything like he used to. Is that the kind of Jesus we want – as good as dead? Is that the Jesus of the Gospels, or only the one in the grave? Nearly 500 years ago, Michelangelo carved his Pietà out of a great piece of marble. This magnificent sculpture stands in St Peter's in Rome. It shows a dead Jesus lying helplessly on his mother's lap. This is a wonderful work of art – but it is not the biblical Jesus.

Explosion of Life

If Christ is risen, we want to see some living evidence of it – especially when we come together in his name. If we don't come to church to meet a living Jesus, then why do we come? Are we there to be entertained; to look at fine art; to soak up the atmosphere; to listen to the rumbling organ and the pure voice of a choirboy echoing in the vaulted roof; for the twanging of guitars and the clatter of drums – or for some other bit of showbiz?

A preacher who loved the sound of his own voice once found a note waiting for him in the pulpit one Sunday. It was a quote from one of the Gospels: 'Sir, we would like to see Jesus' (John 12:21). For the preacher, this was like a slap in the face. It made him realise what he was there for – to preach Jesus, and not to serve up lofty philosophy. A month later, he found a second note in the pulpit. It was another quote from John's Gospel, and simply read: 'The disciples were overjoyed when they saw the Lord' (John 20:20). The preacher had obviously got the message!

THE VACANT GRAVE

If you read the sermon of Peter in Acts chapter 2 at the beginning of this book, you will see that the only occupied tomb he mentioned was King David's. He never argued that the tomb of Jesus was empty. He had no need. Everyone knew it. They all knew that the body of Jesus had completely vanished. If Jesus had still been lying there, a shrouded corpse, it would have been very different. They would have laughed at Peter and said: 'You fool, Jesus is dead! He's still there in the cemetery – go and see!'

But nobody said that. Nobody could produce him. His friends would have done so if they could. So would his enemies, to prove that he was dead. In all that vast crowd on the feast day in Jerusalem – at the very time when the details could be checked, those involved interviewed, and all the facts known – not one person came forward to contradict anything.

Peter called them 'fellow Jews and all of you who live in Jerusalem'. He was talking to a mixture of pilgrims and local people. He couldn't get away with fudging the facts, because the local people knew everything that went on in the city. They knew that what Peter was saying about Jesus was all true. This is why they were 'cut to the heart' (Acts 2:37). Not one of them could deny that Jesus was alive. Peter could talk plainly about the resurrection, without any fear of heckling from the vast crowd. He said: 'But God raised him from the dead, freeing him from the agony of death, because it was impossible for death to keep its hold on him. Therefore let all Israel be assured of this: God has made this Jesus, whom you crucified, both Lord and Christ' (Acts 2:24, 36).

In Jerusalem, there is a place called the Garden

Tomb. There is very strong evidence that this is the place where Jesus was buried by Joseph of Arimathea, and where he rose from the dead on the third day. Pilgrims sitting there often feel a strange and powerful sense of relief stealing over them. Men and women find tears in their eyes. The doorway to the little cave in the cliff face is almost like a mouth, declaring the good news of Easter: 'He is not here. He is risen. All is well.'

Take this event out of history and it all collapses into unpatterned chaos. That is just how many people in the modern world see our existence – it is all meaningless. In the face of this futility, people lose hope and sink into despair. But if Christ is risen, it all starts to add up, all the way from Adam. The message to the whole world, lost in despair and darkness, is this: 'If you confess with your mouth, "Jesus is Lord", and believe in your heart that God raised him from the dead, you will be saved' (Rom 10:9).

'I am the resurrection'

Standing outside the tomb of his friend Lazarus, Jesus spoke with Martha, Lazarus' grieving sister. But his words were much more than the comforting words which people try to offer each other at funerals. His words were stunning in their power and authority. He said: 'I am the resurrection and the life' (John 11:25).

This is a remarkable statement. How can Jesus be the resurrection – how can he be an event? The problem here is that we think of the resurrection as an event, but the Bible speaks of it as God's power. Resurrection is actually the 'eternal life' Jesus spoke about, and eternal life is the life of God himself. This resurrection (or life-giving) power was at work throughout the ministry of Jesus, as he healed the sick, gave sight to the blind, cast out demons and raised the dead. But we can see God's power at work most clearly in the resurrection of Jesus himself. Peter,

Explosion of Life

in his sermon on the Day of Pentecost, said that 'it was impossible for death to keep its hold on him' (Acts 2:24). In fact, it would have been impossible for death to take hold of him in the first place, but Jesus surrendered himself to death.

He said, 'No one takes my life from me, but I lay it down of my own accord. I have authority to lay it down and authority to take it up again' (John 10:18). Jesus went to the cross seeking death as a warrior seeks out an enemy.

John's Gospel tells us how he died: 'When he had received the drink, Jesus said, "It is finished." With that, he bowed his head and gave up his spirit' (John 19:30). In this verse, the normal word for dying is not used. Instead, Jesus deliberately gave up his spirit to God. What does this tell us? It tells us that Jesus invaded death and hell to conquer them. Death did not conquer him. When Jesus came he put his mighty shoulder against the gates of death and burst them open. The Bible describes this by picturing him as a conquering warrior: 'When he ascended on high, he led captives in his train and gave gifts to men' (Eph 4:8).

Jesus said: 'I am the way and the truth and the life' (John 14:6). Wherever he is, there is resurrection power. Whatever he touches comes alive. Wherever he walks, life follows. It is by him that one day the dead will be raised. He is the fountain of all resurrection life. Look at these statements by Jesus: 'I have come that they may have life, and have it to the full' (John 10:10). 'I tell you the truth, he who believes has everlasting life' (John 6:47).

Jesus was not talking about physical life, which we share with the animals, but the fullness of life which only God can give us. Physical existence is all right for creatures that nourish a blind life in their brain and have no real self-consciousness. But human beings were created to rise higher than this. We can discover this life for ourselves if we choose the gift of life which comes through Jesus Christ alone. When we turn to him, the power of his resurrection flows from him to bring us the healing and wholeness which God longs to give us. 'As the Father has life in himself, so he has granted the Son to have life in himself' (John 5:26).

Jesus Christ was not just any ordinary dead man whom God selected at random to raise to life. As the Son of God, the power that raised him from death was also in him. He contains all the resurrection power there is. It is to him alone that we can turn to receive new life. As Peter said to Jesus: 'Lord, to whom shall we go? You have the words of eternal life' (John 6:68). And as the great hymnwriter, Charles Wesley, wrote: 'Thou of life the fountain art'.

SHOCKED INTO LIFE

A colleague of mine once told me about one of his boyhood escapades in the days before electricity came

Explosion of Life

to ordinary homes. Each morning at 7 o'clock he delivered newspapers along a road of wealthy houses. One of them, the very largest house, had an electricity supply. At the door there were two large brass bells, one inside and one outside the porch. This was too inviting to a boy of twelve, and he used to ring both bells each morning – despite angry protests from the residents.

One morning the bell push itself was alive. The boy had a shock which numbed his arm. It also made him a hero. He boasted at school of an electric shock, which nobody else had ever experienced.

A day or two later, fascinated by the electricity that had made him the talk of the playground, he decided to experiment with the bell. He found a length of strong steel wire, and worked out a plan to make the current pass down it. It was raining as he walked towards the bell with the wire held in his wet hand, waving around three yards ahead of him. Before he was ready for it, the waving wire made contact. He almost turned somersaults with the ferocity of the shock!

Soon afterwards, he went into a Gospel service for the first time. He had no more acquaintance with the Gospel than with electricity. He had been brought up to believe that churchgoers were either fools or frauds. Full of prejudice, he sat there listening. He started to notice that the people around him were smiling, as if they were sharing a secret joke. Light sparkled on the gold-rimmed glasses of a nearby old woman, and it seemed to spark and dance along the rows of the congregation.

The last hymn was being sung, when suddenly, like the wire hitting the bell, something electrified him. He said, 'It was as if Christ came and said, "I want you."' At only twelve years of age he became 'activated' for God. He remains activated to this day. His experience is not unique. Many, many people have met the risen, living Christ in similar ways.

A FIRST-HAND FAITH

Nobody knows what it is like to meet Jesus and to experience his resurrection power until they do so for themselves. Onlookers cannot imagine it. Meeting Jesus can never be a second-hand experience.

This experience has been part of the Christian faith from the very beginning – dating right back to the Day of Pentecost, where this book started. Early that morning, the men and women followers of Jesus, including the disciples and Mary, his mother, had gathered together in the upper room where Jesus had eaten the Last Supper. Suddenly, the power of the resurrection fell upon them. The Holy Spirit, appearing in the form of fire and wind, filled them and transformed their lives for ever.

Filled with the Holy Spirit, the believers began to

speak in other languages. The crowd which gathered to see this extraordinary sight included pilgrims from many different countries who were in Jerusalem for the feast. Amazingly, they could hear the good news about Jesus in their own language.

Sceptics in the crowd explained it all by saying, 'These people are drunk!' (Acts 2:13). How else could outsiders explain it, when they had never tasted it for themselves? When Paul, an intellectual, met the risen Christ, he fell to the ground and was temporarily struck blind. Later he was accused of being 'beside himself, mad'. Even Jesus was said to be 'out of his mind' by his own family (Mark 3:21). These accusations are quite understandable — but completely wrong! The only people who know the real effects of resurrection life are those who have been 'quickened' by it, as one version of the Bible puts it — or 'made alive' (see Eph 2:5).

THE RESURRECTION PEOPLE

We have seen from the Gospels how Jesus constantly promised to give his followers new life. After the Gospels, the next book is the Acts of the Apostles. Its very first words refer to 'all that Jesus began to do and teach'. Began! While here on earth, Jesus only *began* his work. Acts shows how he continued after his resurrection and ascension.

This dynamic book tells us how the same works of Jesus reached people everywhere, in ever-increasing numbers. How did this happen? It happened through the disciples' hands, which became the hands of Christ, and their voices, which became the voice of Christ. The power of the resurrection in Jesus flowed from him through ordinary people. They were his channels.

One of the most striking characters in the early chapters of Acts is the apostle Peter. Peter shows us what the power of the resurrection can do to a broken person. When Jesus was arrested, Peter simply went to pieces. At the Last Supper he had said that he would go to prison with Jesus – and even die with him. But later that evening, at the house where Jesus was being interrogated, a servant girl asked Peter if he was a follower of Jesus. Peter cursed, and swore that he never even knew Jesus.

Then the crucifixion took place. Three days later, the women reported that they had seen Jesus alive. This must have scared Peter more than ever. If the authorities heard the rumour, they would be sure to round up everyone connected with Jesus. Peter was the leader of the disciples. He and they shut themselves away behind locked doors for safety.

Six weeks later, on the Day of Pentecost, Peter was dramatically changed. Fear left him and burning boldness took its place. It wasn't only seeing the empty tomb, or meeting the risen Christ – what finally

Explosion of Life

transformed him was the power of the resurrection flowing into him through the Holy Spirit.

Jesus himself had promised them: 'I tell you the truth, some who are standing here will not taste death before they see the kingdom of God come with power' (Mark 9:1). Peter should have been terrified by what happened next on that morning of Pentecost. The disciples could not hide any more. They were discovered. A vast crowd surged upon them. It may have contained people who had howled for Jesus to be crucified.

But Peter came out into the open. He stood with the other eleven apostles and preached without a trace of his old fear. Only weeks after denying Jesus, only days after hiding behind locked doors, he was now willing to own him before the whole world. Soon it was the crowd that was afraid – not the disciples.

Behind Peter's words was the resurrection power that had raised Jesus. Like laser-controlled weapons his words found their mark. That day saw something that had never been seen before in all history: three thousand people turning to God and finding salvation.

Now there was a new sort of people on earth: resurrection people. From the outside they looked the same, but within them they carried the life of Jesus. They knew him, obeyed him, and loved him. When they acted in the name of Jesus, the power of the resurrection was released. They started to see miracles taking place – just as Jesus had worked miracles during his ministry.

CHAIN REACTION OF LIFE

What happened to Peter and the disciples that day long ago still happens today. The Bible describes it in this way: 'If anyone is in Christ, he is a new creation; the old has gone, the new has come!' (2 Cor 5:17). Jesus described this new beginning with these famous words: 'No one can see the kingdom of God unless he is born again' (John 3:3).

When someone repents and believes in Jesus, he or she becomes a new creation, a child of God, and is born into eternal life, just as the Bible promises. Born-again people are different. They are different inside, because the Spirit of God now lives within them, making them 'living temples' of the Spirit (1 Cor 6:19–20).

They are also different on the outside. Not that they look any different – haloes are not included! But Christians are different in the way that they live. As Jesus said: 'Let your light shine before men, that they may see your good deeds and praise your Father in heaven' (Matt 5:16). Paul talks about the richness of the resurrection life, which we carry around in our mortal bodies: 'We have this treasure in jars of clay to show that this all-surpassing power is from God and not from us' (2 Cor 4:7).

Explosion of Life

He goes on to explain the ways in which the resurrection life makes a difference to us: 'We are hard pressed on every side, but not crushed; perplexed, but not in despair; persecuted, but not abandoned; struck down, but not destroyed. We always carry around in our body the death of Jesus, so that the life of Jesus may also be revealed in our body' (2 Cor 4:8–10).

The power of the resurrection opens up to us God's tremendous spiritual resources. It made the first Christians unsinkable – like the proverbial cork, always somehow coming out on top – and it will do the same for us too. A historian said about the early church: 'They outlived the heathen, out-died the heathen, and out-thought the heathen.' They still do!

Explosion of Life

When Jesus was raised from the dead in that tomb, it was an explosion of life. Waves of spiritual power have continued to bring new life to millions of people ever since.

Words alone cannot do anything to change people. For myself, I preach in the simplest and most direct terms the good news of Jesus, the crucified and risen Saviour. I do my job, and Jesus by the Holy Spirit does his work. He walks among the crowds and everything happens. The sick are restored, the blind see, the deaf hear, the disabled walk, and demons are sent packing. Thieves repent and confess. The police have sometimes not had enough storage space for the stolen property returned.

The apostles became walking wonders. Early in the book of Acts, Peter and John healed a man who had never been able to walk. The event stunned everyone who heard about it – including the temple authorities, who were horrified that the work of Jesus was going on. They arrested and interrogated Peter and John, but what struck them even more than the healing was something else: 'When they saw the courage of Peter and John and realised that they were unschooled, ordinary men, they were astonished and they took note that these men had been with Jesus' (Acts 4:13).

And it didn't stop there. Saul of Tarsus, a Jewish religious teacher, grew to hate the first believers. His hatred outshone all the other enemies of the church. 'Breathing out murderous threats', he launched a vicious campaign against this fast-growing 'heresy'. He threw all his energies into putting these 'Christ is alive' fanatics into prison.

But suddenly he himself also met Christ alive. He came face to face with the resurrection and the life – and his life was transfigured. Saul, or Paul, as he was renamed, carried out a one-man invasion for the Gospel of the Middle East and Europe. He set in motion a wave of Christian change.

Hunted, beaten, jailed, shipwrecked, stoned and left for dead, the resurrection energies within him made him invincible. What was his explanation? 'I no longer live, but Christ lives in me,' he once wrote (Gal 2:20). He told the Christians in Colossae about 'being strengthened with all power according to his glorious might so that you may have great endurance and patience' (Col 1:11).

These were not empty words. They reflected Paul's experience in the everyday realities of life, and they are true for all Christian believers. Paul did not have a dead religion – paying polite respects to God once a week. He lived a resurrection life. It had started. One after another – sometimes as individuals, sometimes whole families, sometimes in their hundreds or thousands – people received resurrection life. It was as if Jesus himself was there – in Jerusalem, a temple beggar, born lame, leaps to his feet; in Samaria, paralysed people are healed, blind people see for the first time, possessed madmen are set free, and many people discover the new life of Jesus; in Cyprus, the Roman governor believes; in Asia Minor, Gentiles hear Paul's message and embrace the new faith; in Greece, the jailer who had imprisoned Paul and Silas for the night is shaken into faith in Jesus by an earthquake, together with all his family; and so on – to Rome, Ethiopia, northern Africa, Spain – to the ends of the earth.

THE RESURRECTION STARTS TODAY

It seems an odd thing to say, but if we are born again we are in the resurrection already. We might think that eternal life starts when we die and go to be with Christ, but in fact, eternal life – the life of the resurrection – breaks into our lives here and now. It is as though we have something of heaven in advance!

Explosion of Life

Jesus' own words are: 'Whoever comes to me I will not cast out' (John 6:37). If we are not cast out, then we are drawn in. As Paul says so often, we are 'in Christ' – and he is 'the resurrection and the life'. The Bible also talks about dwelling or abiding in Christ, 'who is our life'. While we abide in him our spiritual environment is eternal life.

That is why Christians never talk about Jesus as a mere memory. Not even the disciples did – and they had lived with him. For example, they did not weep when they watched him ascend out of sight on Ascension Day. Instead Luke records that they returned to Jerusalem, and after the Day of Pentecost they worshipped in the temple and were filled with great joy (see Acts 2:42–7). They already knew the reality of what Jesus had promised: 'I will be with you always, to the end of the age' (Matt 28:20). They didn't have to invent elaborate religious rituals to make Jesus seem near. He was near. They didn't show a shadow of nostalgia for 'the good old days'. They realised the days were now even better. The victory of the cross had been won, and it brought triumph over death, the world and the Devil.

Best of all, they had received the Holy Spirit. Paul describes him as 'the promised Holy Spirit, who is a deposit guaranteeing our inheritance until the redemption of those who are God's possession' (Eph 1:13–14). The word Paul uses here for 'deposit' is the same word that was used for 'engagement ring' in the ancient world. The Holy Spirit gives us, in this life, a foretaste of the eternal life to come.

Now that the Holy Spirit era has dawned, God's resurrection energies are let loose. They are not confined to one time or place. They do not depend on special buildings, religious relics or ceremonies, nor on a holy city or even a holy land – but as Jesus said, 'where two or three come together in my name, there am I with them' (Matt 18:20).

OPENING THE DOORS

The three years that the fisherman Peter spent with Jesus turned him into a natural theologian. His sermon at Pentecost was a masterpiece of biblical theology, with strong echoes of the way Jesus himself handled the Scriptures. He said: 'God has raised this Jesus to life, and we are all witnesses of the fact. Exalted to the right hand of God, he has received from the Father the promised Holy Spirit and has poured out what you now see and hear' (Acts 2:32–3).

Peter brings together the three great truths of the resurrection which we have been looking at – and he is also the first Christian preacher to bring together all three persons of the Holy Trinity:

God has raised Jesus to life.

Explosion of Life

Jesus has been exalted to highest place of all – the Father's right hand.

Jesus pours out the Holy Spirit upon his followers.

What does all this mean for us? The resurrection is not a 'take it or leave it' belief. Whatever we decide to do about this risen Jesus, it will make a difference to our lives. This is because the resurrection is about life itself. Saying 'yes' or 'no' to life is a very serious matter.

People are sometimes amused by 'religious enthusiasts' who try to persuade them to believe that Jesus rose from the dead. But the question of how we respond to the risen Jesus is a question that will not go away. Something has to be done about it because Jesus is alive – like it or not – and waiting on our doorstep. 'Here I am!' says Jesus. 'I stand at the door and knock. If anyone hears my voice and opens the door, I will come in and eat with him, and he with me' (Rev 3:20).

Jesus stands before the different doors in our lives. He knocks on the door to our homes, our work, our thoughts and feelings – on the door to our most secret, inmost selves. And he asks to be let in, so that his life, light, power and joy can fill us with all the fullness of God himself. How will we respond to him?

In St Paul's Cathedral in London, a famous painting

by the artist Holman Hunt shows Christ as the light of the world. He stands patiently outside a closed door. There was one detail which Hunt said he could not show: the handle. It is on the inside.